CHAOS OF THE IDEAS

William Schomaker

ISBN 978-1-105-10188-5

To all the people who buy this book out of the desire to own another book.

Contents

Spiral

This is the life; a tragic spiral of
Events that spawns a pain that
Continues to be internalized, for reasons of
Safety. No one will ever know how much
It hurts; the chaos of the ideas and
Feelings is frightening as well as spectacular.

Taking every day at a time; walking through
The shadows, all that can be seen is
Pessimism and suffering, and the
Whole wide world ignores it, and
Treats those with compassion like
Freaks and lepers; the nice ones
Always finish last.

Illusion of Patience

Alone is the shadow of
A life wasted by hiding
Behind the mask; an unfortunate
Response to inadequate stimulus. Natural
Excitation impossible to control, and
Unacceptable thoughts pushing the mind
To the edge between society's
Obedience and desired social destruction.
Turning away from the task of finding relief in this construct of provisional perversion is an impossibility in a world full of probable solutions and co operations.
Total attachment to hope aside,
A full answer to the dilemma at hand is not feasible.
Contrary to existence is all
That is plausible.

Time is an illusion of
Patience; a construct designed to
Limit options. The mind is
Forced to choose between the
Moment of a lifetime. The
Essence of this physics constant
Is degeneration; entropy rules the
Landscape of our decisions each
And every day. How we
Accept the entropy is how

We live our lives; to
Decide between waiting and taking
Action, or to choose between
Control and chance. With the
Exception of death, there is
No escaping this decision.

To wait is the idea
Of patience everlasting; to accept
An ideal where life can
Continue forever if led by
One who follows a standard
Path. To believe that death
Will not occur by chance,
But by construct,
And that all is universally
A single plan, with every
Event occurring for a reason,
whether it be designed by physics,
Divinity, or mortal mind. Ignorance
Rules this belief, for chaotic
Implication has no knowledge of
Time; we only experience it
That way; so any single
Moment that could be immensely
Effective to changing the path
Has no logical establishment; weakness
Prevails to accept control over
Probability.

Chance is the proper solution
To living; entropy cares not
For hope or structure. The
Flow of life is constant,
and randomness can lead to great moments of triumph,
Tranquility, and joy, or bring
Down the greatest in their
Fields with a single misplaced
Breath and a syncopated heartbeat.
There is no better way to live than by letting Fate and motion rule over all options;
No man that follows control
Will ever find true happiness
Or proper disgrace, and will
Never seek a higher purpose.

All that is can not
Always be; humanity will make
Its own decisions as both
A whole or as individuals,
But it is the individuals who see outside the ubiquitous.
Death will fall weakly on
The masses, but can never
Ignore a chance to be
Artistic with those that follow
No path; to be outside
The slowly growing room of
Cookie-cutter personalities is what every

Person should aspire to do. Every soul must give up its hold on the future,

So that they never live

The experienced past.

Onanism

Life is but a pleasure to the materialistic peoples who

walk it out of sheer desire, yet without fantasy no person can be truly

happy; all people enjoy releasing their frustrations upon the imaginations of the

lonely. Life a fantasy of human interaction, yet through act of interaction do people find

stimulus; a hearty cinema cannot always quench the thirst of the deprived.

Every act of feeling is a form of self-excitement; there are levels to

ecstasy, even for the virtuous; you must not flog a sinner for their desire to

pet a lamb when you yourself love the feel of wool. This material

fantasy can only be succeeded by a need for the embrace of paper; if you place

value in those who partake in pleasure more readily than you, then aren't you lowering the

value of everything you find worth just the same?

A little death spreads just the same among those on pedestals as it does among those who sanctify

life; so many lives quickly ended one way, but not the other;

the death always equals, but never the same in intensity.

Isn't all pleasure, in reality and abstract, a sin of the flesh?

Accept the Disease; Fear the Order

Life itself is just a shame; everyone pushes
Ambitiously to take what they think is
Theirs. Driving forces of selfishness are
Driving the masses into madness, and
All the world can only be a greedy group of
Imbeciles. Death itself has become taboo, and
Bleeding hearts are treated like they have a
Disease. The heart bleeds, and with every
Drop it's a new reality of pain.

give in; feel it what stops you from
feeling pain compassion is the only thing
you can't sell breathe in the fire;
give up to the shame and be
who you must truly be;
accept those in your reality

Sadness is today's new disorder, and everyone
Quarantines the sick. Breathe the same air as the
Suicidal and you'll get the plague.
Euphoria and lust are designer drugs peddled
On the street corners, so now
Beauty is as thin as paper, and smarts and
Personality are a crime. Inoculated is our world
From its own feelings of depression and guilt.

accept those in your reality; they are the only
friends you'll have that will treat you
human we are all just putty for the
high maintenance class to mold into slaves;
breathe deep some chaos or you will
lose your soul; accept those in your reality
who can truly make you feel whole

The Composition

Standing at the edge of insanity and vanity;
Reaching for the lost ideas of disgrace and disgust that
Hold me to my exultations of originality. Craving
Fear to fall from the clouds like rain from the darkest sky above the
Cities that criticize the free thinking individuals who do their
Best to ease life. a bloody demise for the wicked conformists who shove their ideas down the
spines of the idiots A last call by the damned to all who were
Listening to hear that the world is finally done with
Remembering the dead. all gone are the memories of the martyrs of
change The population rages as life becomes vacant in institutions of
Thought and places of celebration; life is but a
Word describing the animals crying to justice from the sinners who
Provoke a negative feeling. life is death as stated by the
deceased as nature consumes them gladly while trying to fight the
engine of civilization that is known as
conformity Religion of the ruling class rules and produces currency while
Zealots fight back with claims that support their deity's lamentations.
Bright lights fall upon the eyes of those who stepped outside to
Watch a fireworks show that brings them to their knees and blows their little
Minds. a war without any ammo is better than a
peace where everyone despises the guy with the biggest cock

Censorship of new ideas begets a new approach to negotiating trade with the

Warlords in Hell that are willing to kill so their commodity sells.

let's rape all their women and breed a new species of demon while zealots on

both sides aren't looking we'll birth our own army of hellions

A happy day will arise where celebration will be for the

New thoughts flowing from the young generation of

Scholars who've found out how to kill their progenitors. a fire burns beneath

all the world with such life that the spinning of the planet is created by the

walking gods among us End all the madness; vices pushing all the

Virtuous cowards back to when they could comprehend the lasting effects of

Shackles. Why set goals when consequences aren't considered for when you fail because

Creativity wasn't on the agenda? a life below the table listening and giggling at the motherfuckers

who thought that they could be smarter than the youth that they pamper with a

free education It's a shame they won't listen to the voices the of the nonconformists because

Vanity is how they maintain their fucked morality.

a composition of insanity produced when the

composed lies meet the original truth

To The Gutter

So I've discovered that no one
Notices me, and it is quite
Disturbing to see this world
Degenerate into a fierce society of
Beauty and stupidity. sex and pleasure
Rule this community of actively wanting
Idiots; a world where you can't get far
On intellect and skill, but that's just
Fine if you have a pretty face, or a
Muscular build you can get what you
Want; you just have to show up.

Life itself is daunting, but when you are as
Ugly as me, you can't exactly go out and ask
For what everyone else gets; the pretty
People deserve the best, and as for the rest,
We are shoved to the gutter like slime. It's
Maddening that no one looks for a
Talented person; soon this will be a
Thoroughly destroyed world.

As I wake up in the morning, I wonder what
I am going to do next, and when I look for
Attention and love, all I get is hatred and
Pain; a world full of shame and disreality.
If you think you can avoid this, then go do

What I do; write for the changes that you want
To pursue, and when you are chastised for being
Emotional, then fight yourself a hold to hide in.

A dead-minded world is what is now, and all the
Little things that everyone used to care
About are lost in this sea of desire and sin;
Drowning are the people who look towards a
Place of power and fame that can be gained by
Shameless excursions into the soul, and when
I see that dream get crushed, I try to cry, but
Can't release a single tear, because I've been
Trained to show no weakness; the world has already
Decided what it is going to do with me when my
Time comes. This is total stupidity.

When my day comes, I'm ending my life; I will be a
Martyr for the ones who are trying to be something that is
Truly better than the ignorant society that
Plagues the earth, and with my last breath, before I
Stain the wall behind me, I will scream at the top of my
Lungs, begging for a chance to be something real and
Believed in by the revolving existence; the cycle will have
Finally won, and taken me down.

Cry, Beautiful, Cry

The stars come out; the moonless sky calls
For redemption. Darkness alive; every person can feel
Tonight coming down on them; life is an endless
Wonder when the night makes it look like a shining star.

Breathe in the starlight; who needs a
Moon anyway? If the sun rises sooner than
We expected, don't you worry; no one will see tonight.

Promise pain everlasting if we cannot
Shine tonight; it won't be alright if the
Moon is gone from the sky;
Cry beautiful darkness, cry.

Revolving Orb

Moving through this intolerant world is the
Damned; a desolate wasteland created by the
Inexistent intelligence that plagues the very
Fabric of reality. The soul is damaged by the
Never ending realization that nothing is
Everything, and all the affection in the world
Can't supply the addictions of the needy.

Sadness sweeps over the land like a disease; a
Cloud of locusts that never seems to be
Satisfied with the meal that is the human
Condition; a force that will only consume the
Stability of the psyches of every citizen in this
Desert produced by insane sanity. The revolving
Orb that is the lives of every being that has to
Thrive on formed provisions that rule the very
Minds of the dying is a cynical master of deceit.

Living day by day in a rational world that is only
Rational due to the contract made by every resident
Is a sin against the natural and logical impulses;
A world where no one is allowed without strict
Permission to feed the instincts that rule their
Thoughts, and with every single impulse comes a
Thorough reminder that escape from the body is

Only one step away; the death of another day.

Free yourselves from pain, and give to what you
Feel; there isn't any sin in being human, or in
Being real. You cannot let the things that the
Prudish rule your soul; be whatever you want, and
Don't let the order of this world ever take
Control. The day has come to kill, so bring chaos
From your mind, and let not those without a
Heart take from you this time, or ever again.

Cutting; Living; Feeling

Bleeding from the etchings made in untouched
Flesh, and the red living thing turns black
When exposed; the blood is tainted by the soul.
More and more the dripping, gushing liquid
Runs out of the body; all the feelings of a
Dark, tortured past going from living to dead
Before the eyes, yet they are not forgotten.

The past is but the thing that we carry
Always with us; it's in our blood and soul,
And it will never leave our bodies till we
Release it with one last final breath, and
Slip the razor down our skin like it's the
Freedom we've been craving all our days.

Let the feelings that are inside out, and
Never let go of the memories that breed
Internally the emotions of torture and
Disgrace; all the things you know about the
World at large, they will be freed from the
Prison you've created when you act on them.

Garden Made of Hope

Unholy beings everywhere sucking at my
Soul's stash of decent memories; if this is
Sad to you, then leave the room right now.
Deities of hopeless existence feeding off of
Mindless undead people that think they can
Escape the wrath of the sinking feelings that
Pull them down when they find themselves quite
Lonely in the sanity that they create for
Reasons of an understood nature; repent, and give
Away the lost ambitions of a dreamless sleep, for
contentment is found in the knowledge that the
Skin that is worn by the stupefied masses is only as
Thick as we let it be for them on any given day.

Sadness is a disease, or at least to the ignorant it is
A former emotional state that they revisit, like it's a
Dying family member in a graveyard of broken twisted
Thoughts; this livelihood of lost beliefs is seeded in a
Garden made of hope, and every corner has a web made by the
Spiders in my constant screaming sonambulations.

Burning in the fireplace of disturbing ideations where I keep
My holiest obsessions are the creations of death;
A most pleasant fellow is the harvester, but we don't see each
Other that often anymore due to circumstances of maturity.
This isn't easy for you either, is it? To read the babblings of

The confused and the meaningless is a shame upon the planet that is

Inhabited by the cursed few who find themselves believing all the lies.

Circles Running Whirlpool

Running swiftly in the desert as the
Wind picks up I fall into the dream
Before me rushing on the dust cloud
That heads in my direction; closer
And closer is the destruction of every
Emotion by ending interaction of the
Cells inside the skull quickly with a
Speedy metal short between their sections.
All of sound and light as I fall from
Living in a world of painful memories and
Anti-climatic spirals of despair. Give in
To the whirlpool of destruction; all the
Chaos brings you to the end of living
Swiftly and unjustly without any obstacles.

Circles going round the people in the
Whirlpool; running round the end, circles
Swimming as we try to escape every bad
Emotion by redirecting every feeling;
Showing no one what we feel, and not
Expressing all that comes into our puny
Minds while the spiral just continues,
And all who try to run will only hurt
Themselves in the end; maybe when the
End comes, we will all be gone. Now is the
Time to sing to the heavens for a pardon

From the pain, but prayer will not change
Anything, so maybe hope is just a lie made
Up by people who resist the urge to enter
The darkness in their lives, so they do not
Die so quickly like we do tonight.

Circles running round the pain that
Cloaks the mysterious darkness and
Shame, and when you escape from the
Hurt, come back for me; change the
Course of death around the spiral; whirlpool
Gaining speed and when we go into the tow,
Resist not hoping for help and rescue;
Nothing is going to save us from the end.

Alone, heartBroken, & brainDead

this is my world of horror
a dangerous spiral of chaos
regret
and depression
that feeds on the hopes of others
wishing me to see a better future

When I write out the words that are
Rarely read by my friends and family,
I tend to be scared that they won't be
Accepted because of their
Brash poetic hypocrisy.

a burden that cannot be shared by the
unwelcome insults moving from the
lips of the people closest to me
they don't know that the words can
burn and scar
but the pain still shows when
i choose to display it

I haven't composed in a while,
Not out of fear, but out of inspiration not
Reaching me in the state
Of this current reality.

tuning in to a frequency
as all the walls rush in to
isolate me from the ecstasy that could
exist beyond
the bars of this lonely prison

My mind sits and atrophies in this
Hell that was created for the
Possibly exceptional person
Who would have made it passed the
First obstacle in a social world if
It were not for
The conformity of others.

Man Turn Shadow

The waves of pain excite my imagination,
Pulling me towards the end of sanity so
Much faster; life is but a blur. Giving
Up the honestly painful existence, I
Rush to the dark spot inside my head.
No more heartbeat, and no more breath;
Living is such a conformist existence
Anyway. Planned the bloodshed for my
Dying moments, and all the wounds are
Bleeding steadily into the descending
Spiral that is my flesh in corporeal
Form; I am the mortal coil for the ideas
And inspirations of the dark living
Breathing thing that is the shadows in my
Cloister. Death will be its end for now.

The blood rushes to my brain as every last
Thought exits my skull with hurried momentum;
Rushing forward into the bottomless pit that
Is the internals of my soul now that is has been
Bored out by every vice, sin, and levity in this
Tortured, conformist world created to suffice till
The end takes all. All my vision is turned into a
Dizzying blur, rushing past me like a wind full of
Moisture during the rains that purge me of my
Holes. The skin melts off with burning smell and

Sound; it sickens those who watch me from the
Audience on the other side of reality; there is no
Better entertainment than watching a man turn shadow.

Hanging in the Closet

The noose is hanging waiting for the
Neck in which to strangle; life is a
Ruse, created to fool all who live it.
Being defeated by the pain is something
That all must do some day, and today
Another might; another statistic for
The books; no future in sight.

Life is not there after today, it is
All just words that people say to
Avoid the pain of watching that one
Die, and it is all a lie to tell; no
Person wants to watch a friend become a
Corpse, so they all try to be the friend
That tells them to not worry; that life
Will get better, but if that's true, then
Where is the proof of that?

The answers lie inside the soul; the mind
Translates them. You can't deny that all
The things that come forth are a mystery;
Thoughts and emotions and fantasies of
Lying on that cold table, letting all those
Who didn't do anything cry over you, and
As you lie there, dead and cold, you realize
That they are the ones to blame for your

Loneliness and your complete sadness; the
Visions of living that the crying have are
Just lies if they weep for you; no one could
Predict that seeing through the advice was
Possible all the time it has been told.

So now that you are dead and free, what is
Life in all its glory? Living is
Overrated, and all those that say otherwise
Can die, and find out once their time has come.

Verses of Insanity

I feel the delirium
Filling me inside;
My soul is contained
In a madness reborn.

My delusions are real,
And reality false.
The magic is here,
And the science is lost.

My heart it finds
A new rhythm to beat.
My sin it finds
A darkness alive.

Kill my light;
Extinguish my soul,
So the darkness can take me,
And feed my desire.

The Man from the Shadows

Sitting in his room alone,
The young man wondered
Why he lived in such a dark
And poisoned world, and watching
In the shadows were the things
That scared him. Without a
Doubt in his mind that
Ending everything he had in this
Sad place would bring him peace,
The young man ate the barrel,
And squeezed away the life he had.

Out from the shadows came
A man, and questioning the youth that
Took the most precious gift
That one could get, he
Pulled the round from the corpse's
Skull, and brought the thief of
Punishment back from perdition.
The damned fool blinked his eyes,
But when he saw the dark
Figure before him he shut
Them, and in fear of repercussion,
He panicked and cried,
And screamed in horror.

Then all at once he was
Touched by the pain, and upon
Realizing once more that
He was alive, everything of
Why he died came back.
When the man from the
Shadows saw the look of anguish
On the face of the fool's
Soul, he returned to the
Dark; a fitting punishment
For foolish thievery.

Antenecrophilia

It's depressing; a love like this so
Pure, but innerving; one day, the last
Straw break the camel's back,
And I will be alone.

This is the worst; what could be
Possibly wrong with being aroused by a
Possible end? This is disturbing, but I know it's
Right, and I will not fight
The beauty of a death possible.

If she were to get better, and
Free from this illness, I would
Forget her, because I need a girl
Who is sick like me,
And it is quite scary,
But I'll keep loving death.

So What?

Ladies and gentleman of the audience
Are you hoping for another "song" of
Sadness and despair today? To tell
You the truth I may be depressed and
Suicidal, but inside my head the people
Sing, and when they do it's very loud.

There are parts of me that would like to
Say that if my writing was popular, and I
Wasn't obscure, I'd be getting all the
Ladies and the fame, but right now I'm just
Kept a secret by those who wish to not let
Know that they want an emotional experience
Without consequences; not exactly something
That I restrict from, so all of my emotional
Compositions become an addiction. So what?

All I want out of this world is recognition;
A woman to love me, and a life without
Burden, but since I burden everyone with my
Extensive emotional expressions, I've started
To see that some part of me is becoming more
visceral; I'm losing all of myself to that
Part of me that tends to act as though death
Would be a better choice, because the natural
Tendencies are coming out, and when they take

Control, I will become that guy you don't want to
Know; should that happen to me, or should I escape
the fury of those damned, uncontrollable urges?

Maybe everyone feels this way sometimes, but I can't
Say what everyone feels, after so long without
Affection, so I cry out in my mind; I'm trying to
Quiet down my id as it screams for something more
Visceral in nature; a part of me that I don't want to
Recognize normally, but who is to stop it? The ideations
Of an inappropriate existence may be natural, and
Sometimes kind of interesting and intriguing to
The people that surround me, but I can't just go around
Acting like it's normal for me; I'm too moral, and I
Respect the feelings of others; I try to protect my
Friends and family from the burden I would place if my
Immoral side took control today. Who should I not save?

Virtue of Vice

Place your trust in no one;
Trust only what you see.
Give in not to virtue;
Let vice be your guide,
And care not that you are
Scared and cold, care only
That you get what you desire.
Fight all foes who hold
Your wants, and kill all
Those that stand in your
Way; let not conscience be
Your guide; let your mind
Go completely astray.

Damnation in Reality; Rejection Is Ignorance

All it takes is a couple of well-placed silences
to change what is felt in the hearts of many;
a seemingly beautiful distraction that turns
ugly when assumptions must be made of
intentions. The lack of existing tolerance of a
physical manifestation of humility is a crime
against nature and unity, so choosing
acceptance is an obvious decision to the honorable and kind.

black is the hole in the hearts of the
deformed and socially neglected individuals

Carving good feelings from what appears to be
an acceptance into a more pleasing reality is what the
ugly do; only those who are inwardly ugly can
assume that hurt doesn't exist, but then
the physically displeasing inform them otherwise.
To believe that it is a shame to fraternize with
intelligence and honor is an ignorant
reaction to teachings of equality.

one life isn't worth all others unless
it ends to make a difference

The everlasting cause that all should commit to is

trading appearance for truth; vanity for tolerance.
The world will fail if the imbeciles tend to
breed solely on the desire to become the owners of popularity.

Cigarette or a Gun

This is me; I'm insane; why do you
Care about what I think? All you
Want is for me to consider you when
I'm down; not exactly the nicest thing
To do when I'm having a breakdown;
All the thoughts in my head are spinning.
A cigarette, or a gun; one is going into
My mouth by the end of tomorrow if I don't
Find the answer to why everyone has to
Put me down when I'm already at the
Bottom, trying to crawl my way back up,
But I don't have the strength because
Someone has oiled the walls. Someone please
Free me from this prison created by the
Sane; this doesn't make any sense; why am I
Ignored when I hurt inside? My bad moods are
Everyone's bad day, and it has been decided
That I don't matter when I feel a certain
Way. Kill all the preconceptions about how
Things will go if you react properly; help me
Escape this prison, if you care enough to
Save a soulless bastard who has troubled all
With words of darkness while crossing through
Time; like a traveler who is running around
With no compass. End my pain tonight.

Adventure in the Bedroom

No inspiration; this is damnation; there is no
End in sight. The mind is
Wandering; it's kind of boring,
And this is torture done right.
No entertainment; fed only ignorance,
But blood is rising to the skull.

Life is a cycle of climax and doldrums,
And when you discover this is but a
Story, you will find yourself having an
Adventure; bleeding with the warriors of the past,
So make this bliss last.

Hallucinations breed in the anticlimactic air;
No excitation or change occurs in this
Forgotten universe, and if time and fate
Continue to wage war like this on the
Mind, then maybe it is time to
Conquer life as it has been given.

Fighting monsters that are only fictional beings
That can be seen because the darkness soars
Across the eyes, but defeating
Them will be paradise everlasting.

As sleep comes down, bringing the

Imagination to a much needed rest,
All of the creatures encountered start to
Sleep in the light created by the
Dreams of men, and before the
Moonlight reaches them, they blackout at the edge.

Voices; Days

All the things that are spoken in my
Head are confusing; so many voices at
Once speaking to drive me further into
Insanity, and in an instant I am disabled
By their murmuring. They drive incessantly
To be the loudest voice, even over my own,
But I resist letting them take control.

It's the voices that are telling me to be
The thing so primal in my thoughts, and when
They talk it's like my brain is on the path
To pain. I can't find a love, or any sort of
Ecstasy like they are requesting because it is
An objectification of the women that I want to
Hold dear some day in the near future.

All these voices lead me to my suicidal
Conclusion every day, but I resist for as
Long as I can muster up the inner voice
That like me wants to sing out, and I create
"Songs" of madness that will spill out from
The deepest corners of my mind, showing off my
vision of what is real, and what is just a fantasy.

As the voices hold me down, I cry out for the
End, but it isn't as simple as that; they want

Me to be destroyed by their notions of narcissism
And ideations of a twisted psyche that I refuse to
Allow become a part of my existence at any time;
I try to fight, but I fear that soon I will be
Fighting with myself for control, and then it will
Be my last day in this reality that I have created
Solely for my survival in this wretched world.

Dark Battle

Quaking with the fear established after many
Years of suffering, so now the world looks
Jaded. All the pain and torture a fond memory of
Times of influence; another day can't pass without
A mild recollection. Lost to the thoughts of times
Long gone, and an age when people found joy in
Spite of innocence, but all the living is over.

Rising from the damned orifices created; no escape in
Sight of this place, and running will do no good. The
Corpses of a past unseen, and a future to become are
Ambulating towards the living images that were once
Family and friends, for those are the only things they
Can recognize. This is the night of retribution.

Lifting the blade that has been stricken by the Harvester,
And given the courage to fight, the warriors of this mighty
World prepare for battle with the souls of past acquaintances.
A battle is all that can be accomplished, for this war will
Continue till the end of time, unless by some small feat of
Unimaginable light the damned and perished fall to their knees.

Living in My Head

In here are the delusions that
Dilute the senses that must be
Relied on to have self-control;
Escape is necessary. Breathing in the noxious
Fumes, and intoxicating as they are,
Their poison sweeps the mind away.

This is the truest prison created to make
One think of shadowy, horrible creations to
Torment the souls of others; the lack of
Oxygen creates hallucinations that
Permeate past the imagination.

Living in my head are all the
Lepers and the dead that cannot speak
For themselves, and it is quite crowded
In this dark, torturous place.

Every Little Blade

All the lost breath that is pushed from
These burning lungs of flesh and
Imagination, and all the darkness in this
Underground cavern of sparkling life.
The thoughts of all the delirious are
Seeping down into the earth, and dripping from
The ceiling; we are drowning in their filthy
Ideations. This is but a trap to keep us
Contained; a prison for holding the
Intellectually insane. The time for escape is at hand.

Running out of the prison walls, and every little
Blade of grass is poisoned by our steps; we
Trample nature while we suffer living. The
Lasting impression that we leave is nothing but a
Nasty black spot on the mental status of the
Population; breeding is becoming a game of
Chance, and the drops of life that are the
Dice are fleetingly being wasted by the ignorant.

Free all the wise, and give us our dues; we
Deserve to live like you, and we will fight for
Our rights. The smartest should survive; who cares
If the meek are also smarter than the strong?

Run away! The flood is rushing from underground.

Your mind is vulnerable to the stupidity that is
Growing the earth around us into death, and there is
No deity to worship; the lies are sinning us to the end.

Here the Pill Lies

The colors are bright, and everything is
Textured in this little hallucination I have been
Dropped in by mistake; I can't believe I took that
Purple pill left by my bed in the evening. This is
Like a train wreck created by happiness and fear;
Maybe it will go away if I ignore it, but I can't
Be too sure it is even there; what is going on
Here? Is this the ending creation from the Divine?

Music becomes a visual and tasty creation in this;
Every sound is vibrant and shaded with mystery and
Glory; the ticking of the clock is visible as all
The other sounds follow it, and I can feel the
Parasites that crawl under my skin feeding on my
Joy in this dimension. The feelings here are
Indescribable, but I can see them clearly in my
Vision; where is my sanity that I collected?

The pain is starting to become unbearable! Help
Will not come any closer than the colors, and
The crawling is now a tearing at the flesh; my
Blood is flowing from every wound like water;
My skin is turning black at every orifice created
By the spiders crawling from my body and feeding on
My breath and senses! This is now a horror I couldn't
Imagine! Oh dear living prudes, save me from this!

Making Sense in Fantasy

closing out the day as the sun sets; mind in a
Haze of depression and constant imagery of murderous intentions
That frighten away rational thoughts. Closing are the
Daylight visions of integrity and honor that hold together the
Mind in a temporary structure; where the sanity is gone no
One will seem to ponder. all the emotions breeding instances of
insecurity the killer kindred spirits in the skull are maddening
screaming for some resolution of hope that could come never
death it seems is creeping up the steps of
indecision Taking rationality and sending it
Away are the things that run around inside you
When you least expect them to. Leaving droppings of the
Brain that was digested by the sane; breathing
Sin and sorrow in the gloom. burning are the urges to kill the
masses huddling bubbling are the thoughts that
drive surrender into view and crush all
hope of acceptance by the herds of sheep that
rule the world; ending up a wolf is better

Lying in wait are the mouth-breathing tainted
Thieves of justice; giving power to a snake is wrong.
Lift up the joys of demise for them, and teach them to
Sing in chains. Judged by the afraid, but condemned by the
Tyrants; this world is such a shame. shamefully the sounds of
oppression will grow in strength and rip away the power

from the programmed; sins will grow and take the
day and night will be what's left for the proper
Live in the night, and let you feelings
Soar by the light of the moon. Blood will
Fall from the sacks of shit that we refer to as
superior. liars and cheats that ruin our lives will
die by the hands of the fallen and
crying and madness will reign; rip away the beings of
belief that control our days and
all of our deaths will not be in vain

the blood will be spilled and the winners will
be those with the power to will their own thoughts into
truth Let not all your inhibitions win; kill off
Doubt, and cast away fear. Drink of the wine that
Flows from you enemies' dirty hearts, and be saved.
rationality is gone and all the world will drown in
sorrow; free from chains we will all be and
cries will be heard but our tongues will be still;
we are not one voice to scream but a
cacophony of armed intentions; this is our day but our
night is where we will reign Sadness, doubt, and
Fear are ejected, and all that is left is
Doubt resurrected as courage and bloodshed.

Twisted Future Calling for Mine Lover

In sight is beauty; intoxicating is the
vision. As she walks by, the air around her becomes
Warmed by the glowing light that shines
From her; maybe she will let me bask in that
light. feeling her heartbeat from a distance every
inch of her brings me to my knees begging the
universe please to let me taste her and feed her every
sensual need I am stricken with infatuation as she strolls
By. My thoughts of her are pure as I
Look into her gorgeous eyes, and all the
World stops for a moment while she takes a breath;
I'm losing my mind. is it possible to take her sanity away and
make her cry out in pain for her
body makes me weep so it's time to show her
the way into a future of darkness A life of
Interesting times awaits her; my grasp takes
Her off her feet. time to bring her to
kneel for me begging that it stop before
she cries the pleasure will dull her sense and
poison her mind so she becomes the
little slave I desire She will be the
One who sets my heart aflame every day and
Night; I will hold her tight and keep her safe.
she will be safe from everyone but me when the
sun goes down I will show her how to beg for mercy

Orgasm

The movement jubilation; life it seems is
Moving forward. A smile caused by involuntary
Neurological and chemical activity;
An unbelievable source of pleasure that
Pushes forth inside the soul,
Causing the screaming to roll out the
Mouth like a hunter sounding a call!

A shudder of ecstasy; a moment of full
Pleasure; a full breath of momentary
Agony, then joy in full chemical measure;
A little death created for shared
Carnal knowledge; the only way to
Communicate with a divine being.

Once it's over with, there is
Emptiness, but that doesn't matter, because you
Can hold the other till it goes
Away, then maybe go after it again.

Streaming Affection Only Goes So Far

The world outside is full of shallow women
With high standards, so inside I'm
Dreaming of finding a girl who sees for what I
Am and accepts it. I go out into the stream,
Take out my phrases, and bait a good one.
When I show her my appearance she doesn't run,
And I start to feel like I am someone
With something worth liking. Moments later I
Ask to see the beauty that has chosen me,
But then she runs away like I'm a
Sexual deviant rapist.

you already know what my body is,
so why does it scare you to enlighten me on yours

Am I not what you were looking for?
Do I seem like I lost affection for your
Personality? I may be the kind of guy who's
Willing to show you what he has, but when it's
Only fair to reciprocate you go running scared;
Are you afraid I'll think less of you?

you shouldn't be afraid to show some
skin; if you prefer I'll undress you

Are you prudish? Is your personal space existing
Inside of cyber space? It's not understandable to
Use a man for his body. Do you need some
Time to think, or will you bitch all night
Because you are afraid;
Do you every really want to get laid?

the sky's the limit when you
aren't bound by shame

Heart in a Jar

I go through this world walking in the
Shadows barely noticed by the world around.
My environment a bubble of true insanity, and
All I know a bloody mess of feelings breaching every
Rational desire. I have found that nothing that surrounds me
Makes me feel loved or happy, so I go on seeing
beauty ignore me and my expressions. every
single pretty girl a new infatuation; all the
sexy ladies a new lusting fantasy all the
blood rushes to excite my imagination; love will never
find me but at least I can envision impurity of
every single beautiful woman Love is something that
Evades me; I understand it, but it runs from me at
Every rendezvous. My mind is restless with fantasies of
Connection, but daydreams are all I have when there is no
Attraction. all my heartbeats quicken and I
pump out all my frustrations but the pretty girls don't see me as an
option; continuing to lust with every fantasy I bust
away the nervousness that consumes my soul; all the
love in the world will overlook me until I'm in a hole
I find myself lonely in the shadows, and every killer
Instinct takes me. My goal is not to kill what
Sexually excites me, but to smash the jar and let my
Feelings go into the ether. my heart is in a jar for the
one who finally loves me but I fear that day will

never come; with a final heartbeat I can be free of
imaginary circumstances that are fucking with my ability to
find a mate; all I have are fantasies of desire My
Heart is in a jar to give to you when whoever you are
Comes to me; a true emotional connection that can
Set me free from my insecurities. Affection can be mine when
You finally come to me. without you I will be lost;
lost inside my mental imagery and growing ever weaker at a
cost of spiraling into my end; the end only grows
closer as my constitution falls, and all my
heartbeats leave the echoes of the jar

resonance

a little voice rising among a crowd
of louder than need to be morons
that wish to always be found by
the rest that are like them in
this cold and dramatic world where drama
is a sin that life cannot accept
We of the intelligent and
Unattractive masses respectfully beg and
Request forgiveness from those out
There with beauty and conformity.
individuals are not seen by the masses
of narcissism and desperation to be something
that everyone without would dream to be
All the religions and the media are
Right in their portrayal of goths, dpunks,
And nerds as weaklings and losers looking
For attention by annoying the truly superior.
of course we look for
attention to spread a higher
purpose of thinking for yourself
and avoiding the attraction of
being part of the herd
All of us who keep on
Dying just prove that you are
Better and of course Darwin was

Right because the fittest have survived.
except for the ones who stood in the way of
a shell released on a sad and rainy day when
the meek decided to become the strong and showed the
beautiful masses what death truly brings on for a thought
that assuredly rises is that all are equal in death
so a suicide or silencing of the popular is a
martyrdom for a greater cause that will make us all heard
We are silent.

The Light Goes Dim; the Beast Is Free

The night is a dim lit room full of
Angst and depression; the world unfolds in the
Moonlight. Blood pounding in the brain; sanity barely
Holding in the dark cloak of loneliness, and
Every thought drives the madness deeper into the
Heart. Breathing heavily, but slowly creeping into lacking
Proper judgment; the clock ticks away the control that
Has been holding back the beast within.

growling is the monster in the darkest reaches of
the soul; the moon makes it cry for a feast

All the thoughts are growing colder; the
Light burns the flesh. Rising from its cage of
Horror are the gory shadows. Demons of the
Mind begin to wander freely; the
Heart beats ever faster as the blood runs cold.

look out the window see a beautiful
siren trotting down the road every feeling of
hunger explodes; killer sensations rising up the
spine and pain comes into the mind
driving the body to take her purity away;
end her life and save her for another day

The blood on the hands; a red ink marking the
Beast. Suicidal expressions cannot show the least
Concern for the crimes committed. The body again
Loses all control; the monster is free again, so
All run and hide, or be ripped from existence.

find the siren once again and take her
for a ride; show her love and affection while
she lies still and cold all her thoughts are still
seething in her imprisoned mind; show her
love once more then chew upon her bones

Inedible Rationalization

Cursed by this sleep that never comes, my
Heart is beating oh so fast, and I have no more
Control; running in all directions, aimlessly
Moving towards a bitter end with a sweet after
Taste. This is the last taste of life; it's sweet
Glow and flavor created by the good times, now
Burnt by the times of deceit and pain, and it's
No rational for the ones who can sense the smell
Of burning flesh in this rampant infection called life.

The parasites known as organs can't metabolize this
Poison that tastes like the sweetest wine; it's a
Tragedy I couldn't fix the living condition with a
Little sugar, and the overly sour concoction that came
To be is a creation of lost minds and unholy alliances;
This is the tastiest suicide ever written. Why do we
Continue to consume the death that is mixed by other
Humans, who probably have malevolent intentions? No one
Person wants to help another, unless they lose their sanity,
Or their ability to rationalize morality and legality
Together; the reasons for this new dish are clear.

It's time to toss this painful poison, so go get the
Dumpster full of blackened souls ready; they love this
Inedible trash. This is the final day that any living

Person will ever eat their own heart, and the dead will
Be grateful for that, because they are starving. Feeding
Masses of idiocy is becoming harder and harder, so we
Feed them the dead and damned, but it doesn't fill them
With the nourishment they need, so we can only cry for them.

thoughts among the Screams

i wrote this for you whoever you are a
stranger in the shadows of a time i do
not comprehend as of present
could be my past but my future seems more
likely because i doubt i will ever meet you
My thoughts are vibrant. Insanity
Rampantly runs through my dreams,
And the message is clear
To those who can see.
if you could only hear
what i am saying inside
you would no longer wonder
what drives me to fantasy
I can imagine a world
Where I no longer wear a mask
To hide the true person.
it is anguish in here where the mask covers where beauty
is only an opinion and we all wish that the energy
wasted on hurt could be put to good intentions
for all to see the gorgeous genius that may be here
i am the key to the cipher that is the lie
When I am dead you
Will read a new perspective
That did not
Be until it stole the

Life you selfishly mourn for.

that life is not mine for what you know is not a man but

a character just like you are when you want to be popular and loved except

in this case it is to be to prevent being caged away from all

There is a stranger

That I know who wishes

To hear my thoughts.

and only if they all

knew what this mind goes

through torn by biology and

humanity it is a prison

held shut by a mask

What you see here, ladies and gentlemen, is a new species of primate

Designed by science to exist solely to feel for the rest of us.

not including the writer who created him

Take off his mask!

see the being that is hated by all

of the desired and

loved by the wanting

Rise

This is what we have been
Waiting for; a time of pure
Evolution. Time to fight for
What we believe in; time to
Rise up and revolt against
The oppression of the
Past generations; put aside
The old traditions. Life in
The world can now be given a
New set of values. Rise up
Everyone with weapons made of
Emotion and intellect; we can
Fight those who wish to stop
Progress from happening. Come
To the promised world we want
To live in; rise up and fight
And don't give in to the
Temptation of being allowed
The chance to be a part of a
Society that oppresses those
That want some form of change.
Time for a revolution has
Come and new solutions to the
Problems that plague our
World are here, and if they are

They we will make them be.
Rise up and start the revolution;
We must bring down the former
Institution that holds down each
Day from making the decisions
That will fix the way we live.
Rise up and see the new day.

Rambling Madly Forth; the Killer Ideations

I'm really trying to push pass the
Static inside my mind that stops me
From putting out these compositions.
It's not exactly yielding but I'm
Discovering that it will not win if I
Continue to see what is inside these
Emotions I'm always feeling and I can't
Believe that any one person cares as long
As I am justified to be ignored.

This may be creepy or a little bit
Disturbing to the people all around the
Words are controlling the thoughts;
Emotions are freely guessing as to what
To communicate upon peering and attempting
Comprehension of the words that are written
Here before the eyes. Killer ideations
Take command of living consequences of a
Life that is not living; end it swiftly.

So the static creates a new perspective of
Living in a world where no one really cares,
And yet they say they want to help, but I
Cannot request such things as to brighten my
Life, or end the pain inside the minds of all

The people who read these words carefully;
A sinner interprets them in contrast to a
Bible thumper's accusations of words of evil.
The darkness cannot take what has already been
Sold, so I write this poem in hopes that one
Day I will be allowed to flourish in a world
With no prejudice against the artists.

Chaos grows, but slowly so does order in a
Fantasy created by the masses thinking that
The world as we know it can thrive on what
Is already here taking root. Give in to the
Darkness that you see in front of you at this
Very moment, and when you see what I can see,
And when your perspective has changed, and
Everything is priceless in comparison to you,
Come to terms with your desires; let the
vices set your soul ablaze.

Artificial Nature

Lost in the wilderness of
Mankind's creations are the
Weak; what is this world
That has been deemed as safe?
This is the world in which we
Live and die, and the truth is
There is nothing safe about it
On the lowest levels. Where have
The protectors of the confused and
The broken gone? This is the worst
Assault on the senses; there is
No honor and no chivalry here.
Open up your heart and rise
To fight a war with those who
Destroy nature. Create not a
New world order for it is a curse
Upon this land and planet. There is
No emotion to cause this destruction
But the purest of narcissism and
Greed. Let it fall.

Human Nature Not Disturbing

Rising from the inner depths of the black
Hole inside the heart is a rushing feeling of
Tormented euphoria that quickens the pace of
Horror. flowing from the wounds of time a
soulless monster comes forth breeding violence and
lust for the blood-soaked corpses of the damned Breathe
In the scent of the new order; thoughts are
Free to move themselves. Contagious are emotions of
Destruction; sex and violence feed our empty
Souls. joy comes from blood spraying in all
directions; a mess of decay brings masses of
affection to this dirty reality Vice is rejected no
Longer. Take out the pure and the
Prudish. Let your mind wander into a
New world of sin and shameful choices; unashamed are
We who find peace in the blood. horror rises feeding all the
detached feelings from the population of the
horrid worshipers of lies; feed yourself on
vice and be what was intended by time but
don't let go of your passion let it fly Let your
Passion fly; show the prudish children the
Mind of someone. spinning in a gory horror show of
imprisonment in the skull; breathing air meant to
poison the individuals who revolt from shame
Toxic words will hold you tighter, but take
Away your freedom. Heed the call of your own

Heart, and let no one stop you from feeling
Things that make you real. let go of your
shame and be what you want to be; blood is
dripping from the traitors of human nature

Battle in Hell; Till the End of Time

This is the longest fall that has come to
Pass so far in time, and as all who take the
Trip are ready for the sudden stop, and the
Subtle pain before the fall continues, and
The flames lick the skin as the abyss,
Bottomless and serene, grows ever darker.

This is the greatest journey ever taken,
And there isn't a gate at the front of
Perdition, but there is an army of demons;
The damned and perish their weapons, with
Spears of bone, and bows of fire, we, the
Newly deceased, prepare to fight our way to
Take over the last frontier created for us
To occupy. So, the battle begins.

As we rush forward, the fires blaze at us,
But we are not deterred, and with weapons
Lifted from those we have felled, we fight
With every last breath and inch of skin, with
Every last drop of blood and ounce of virtue
That we have left in our very souls, so as
The demons fall, their master rises to the
Challenge, and with weapons raised, we charge
His blackened and fiery flesh, for we are not
To be his concubines or servants; this is our

Last battle we can fight, and we will conquer
The evil before we conquer Death, and rise
Again to our rightful place as immortals of the
Most powerful; we will fight till the end of time.

Souls of the Ambitious

Burning up everything that is dreadful and
Sadistic; moving through the world that
Powers itself on hate and assumption.
The abyss calls for new residents, but
Heeding the call is a trap, for no one can
Escape alive from the beasts of the damned
Shadow world. Holy beings cry for the lost.

Human blood is the fuel for disgusting
Ambitions of glory and hatred; all those that
Trample on the hearts and souls of the people
That will always be better than them will be
Trapped in the silence set for them after the
Hours have been whiled away destroying the
Lives that set out to be more than usual.

Ungodly chasms await the monsters that possess
The power to condemn the lonely before they
Even end the struggle; the abyss continues its
Call to the damaged. Killer fires rage on in the
Eyes of the soulless living, and the plagued
Throw themselves over the edge into the burning
Mass that is the tortured souls of the ambitious.

There is no warning in this life; loneliness a
Curse for those that seek honor, and

Damnation a punishment for those that seek
Power; the world is but a worthless, burning
Lump of metal and indescribable horror for the
Amusement of the immortals that walk among us.

Every Little Ideation

It is time to let go of the thoughts that
I hold dear; there are no regrets in this
World that I can be accounted for, and
Every little ideation of personal exsanguination is
Just floating in the corner of my psyche, so I try to
Let it go. I can't free myself from my destiny as it is
Right now, because I know of no future for myself
That permits me to go on.

The end draws closer with every breath, and I
Can see no light before me as all of my
Creations in this world are forsaken by the
Living. Now with all my thoughts capable of
Being referenced by title; it is a sad state of
Affairs, and no one person can change how things will
Turn out for this sad soul in the future.

Lost among my creations; all these silly ideations
Take control of me, and I am lost in
Mental arguments with my animal instincts and moral compass;
All the world is at a loss to truly understand me,
So I light another cigarette to salute those that
Are singing with regret. Maybe when this painful
Exposure to the damning fires has passed,
My life will be released.

Exploitation

Living in a shallow pool of darkness are the
Vile creatures that everyone trusts, and it's a
Shame to watch all the good people in the world
Befall to the deception of these beasts
Created by the loopholes in the rules
Society has given us to follow. Exploiting the
Compassion of everyone who wishes to be known for
Helping those in poverty and loneliness; all of the
Good in this world will be drained out by these
Vile things that we let control our world,
And with every drop of human blood that falls due to
Sacrifice by exploitation, one more person is
Born to feed off of the generosity of others.

Isn't it a shame that we let down those that
Really need our help in this world? Isn't it a
Crime to let the truly starving go hungry, so
Others that demand help get fed? It's time to
Let those vile things be pushed down back into the
Muck, and we must take away the luxuries that
Have been afforded them by ignorance and false compassion;
All the "help" they need is just because they cannot
Survive on their own without stealing what is necessary to survive.

Lack of Brain

Losing the thoughts in a sea of twisting
Images that are demented by the blood burning
In your lungs; singing songs of madness we are.
Breathing in the vapors that can turn the best
Men mad, and it's sickening to see the vomit from
The weak and sensitive. Fires are living in the
Souls of the dying, and no one can seem to be
Crying out for any mercy from the harvester.

Run from the damned, for they are the masters of
This place that we call lunacy, and we will do
Their bidding till the end to time; the advancing of
The clock is maddening in sound. Ticking away the
Hours of our lives is like sucking down a poison for
The purpose of killing off the brain cells we don't need.

Suckle on the pipes of ignorance and wrongdoing you
Scum; this is the end of your coming of days.
Believing in a deity that graces you with immortality
Is such a disgrace to human intellect that no one will
Believe you have a brain. Death will come, and take what
He had given you; a life that you did not pursue, and every
Wasted minute that you used for virtue and other luxuries.

Sanity Is Not the Key; Tonight

The night has come; live in the
Moment where you had the most fun,
But find you way; find yourself a
Little excitement in the disarray
That causes life to be so interesting;
There is nothing like a anxious
Moment on a starry night, when the
Rain comes down, take yourself away to
That place where you find that you have
No more reservations; give in to the
Inclinations of a new chaotic fun time.

Come on; stand up and see the pleasure
That you can have from going place that
You've been, and when it comes down to
It, you will have the time of your life;
Nothing like you felt before, and probably
Never feel again, but why does that matter,
When everything is now, and not in the past
Or Future; the experience is all that matters,
And if you can see it in the fray of chaos
Maybe you will find the urge to drop your
Reservations, and all you inhibitions.

Party now; nothing like this will ever happen

After tonight. Every action is the lasting
Memory of what you want, and when you let go
Of fear and shame the world remains spinning
When you see that sanity is not the key to
Happiness and contentment; the only way you
Can go to where you feel yourself alive is
By taking chances on the things you didn't
Think were worth it in the end. Now's the time;
Give in to this lively chaos instead.

Dreams of the Grotesque

Part 1: Introduction to Miranda

The night was cold in the wide expanse of desert that Nathaniel Jones had decided to build his impressive estate on. Traveling there was murder; too much road to drive, and too much dust to deal with for just a friendly little party among acquaintances. Arriving tonight would be just a few people; Nathaniel didn't know too many people that lived in town, but those he did know were some of the most knowledgeable and distinguished, but also the most secretive, strange, and obscene.

The first guest arrived about 15 minutes early, which is

usual for someone of her attitude towards tardiness. Abigail Lemming was a very strange woman, but she made up for it with a skill in languages, and that skill is the reason she visits Nathaniel tonight. Not even 5 and a half feet tall, but quite voluptuous and young, she is the pride of the town's intellectuals, being that she has lived there most of her life, leaving only to go to college, and of course short trips to many different foreign countries to practice her particular skill. Nathaniel greeted her at the front door himself, and brought her inside to the parlor quickly. He handed her a new book he had just acquired in Italy, and headed back to his study, leaving her to entertain herself with Italian literature.

Samuel Denny arrived next, about a minute past the expected time, wearing his usual trench coat, fedora, and black leather gloves, as well as his crisp black suit. Samuel worked at the mortuary; selling caskets to the living was particularly easy for him, as was spending the money he made doing it on the impressive numbers of woman that crowded around him during his nightly follies and entertainment. Many of the men in the town believed that Samuel was a very dangerous man, and hoped that none of their significant others were seeing him secretly. Nathaniel's daughter Emily let Mr. Denny in shortly after he rang the doorbell, and escorted him to the parlor, leaving him to have a smoke while observing Miss Lemming reading the book Nathaniel had handed her.

Arriving only about 4 minutes after Samuel, Marcus Darlow felt he had accomplished himself at being the last guest to arrive. Marcus was the manager at the town bank, and felt himself to be one of the greatest accountants alive. He simply loves numbers, leaving them only second to food, his great bulging stomach under his tight-fitting suit being proof of this. He loved to eat, especially when he had cooked the food himself, and never turned away a free meal when lunch came around. He had just finished an exceptionally prepared sirloin, and was quite ready to have dessert and coffee at the Jones estate. Emily let him in after he knocked loudly at the front door, and took him to the parlor to join the other guests.

Upon hearing the heavy footsteps of Marcus down the hall from his study, Nathaniel came into the parlor as quickly as possible to be a good host, and to entertain his guests himself. He calmly rushed Emily out, and lightly closing the door behind him, he began to speak.

"Welcome everyone. I hope you all safely traveled down my road to my luxurious and well-sized home out here in the hot and unforgiving desert. As you know, I enjoy my privacy, and I only wished to bring all of you out here to me for a very important and amazing discovery I made whilst walking down one of the old trails that extends from about half a mile down my road all the way to the greener parts of the desert on the other side of the town."

The group was looking quite bored at hearing about another one of Nathaniel's discoveries. He was a zoologist by schooling, but at a very young age had inherited quite a bit of money from a very distant and much disowned uncle. Often he would find all sorts of insect and reptile life in the desert while walking down the old trail, but never was it any sort of thing that would be worth mentioning as an incredible or important discovery, and now his acquaintances looked as though they were about to be bored out of their minds. Nathaniel ignored their dirty looks at him, and continued with his improvisational lecture to a very uninterested set of students.

"I was down by the dunes while walking the trail when I saw it. It was causing a group of wild pigs to run wildly about, like they were afraid of it, but I knew that whatever it was, it couldn't possibly be harmful or dangerous, so I caught the creature in one of my specimen jars and brought it back here. Upon further examination of the creature, I discovered it had some sort of gland in it that, when pressed through the skin, emitted a quickly-evaporating substance upon the creatures skin. I exposed some of the mice I keep in my study to the substance, and noticed that they too were having trouble resisting the urge to cower, squeal, and even be violent to one another, until of course eventually they all died. Upon autopsy of the mice I discovered that they had died of no cause whatsoever, like they had just stopped living. So, tonight, I wish to show you all the creature I had found, nay, discovered in the desert, so that you may tell me what you think it is"

He place a small cage on the table in front of the guests, in which was a small, blue, feisty creature with solid black eyes and six limbs. Its slightly scaly skin was glistening, as though it was wet, and it looked at the group with extreme curiosity. Nathaniel tossed a piece of bread into the cage, and the creature ate it quickly, revealing small, fang-like teeth inside its mouth. Abigail looked slightly frightened by the creature, whereas Samuel and Marcus were eyeing it with the same curiosity it was showing towards them, and noticing this, Nathaniel continued with his anecdotal pseudo-lecture.

"I have been studying her for quite some time now, and discovered her to be some sort of parasitic creature with a very omnivorous diet. I have fed her many a food item to discover her diet, and she seems to eat green plants as well as raw meat, but she is quite partial to the meat, and has attempted to bite me quite a few times, but I have evaded her teeth. As for what appears to be moisture on her skin, it is actually the aforementioned substance, which has both hallucinogenic and sedating properties. Hopefully, I may be able to catalogue and display this creature to further generations of scientists, but I can't seem to find a male anywhere in the vicinity of where I found her, so I called you all here to help me identify the possible species or genus of this particular little creature that I have lovingly named 'Miranda'."

Upon hearing her name, Miranda looked up dotingly at Nathaniel, as though she were begging for a treat, or some affection, which caused a mild disturbance among the guests. With the possibility of Mr. Jones keeping this odd, possibly harmful creature as a pet now apparent, the guests were afraid for their own safety. Nathaniel had described as parasitic, meaning that it might possibly be causing him harm, and Marcus was the first to address this possible problem, and advise the group of a solution.

"If this creature is parasitic, then is it truly safe to keep it alive, and noticeably as a loved pet in your home Nathaniel? What if it escapes from its cage and attacks you, or your daughter, or your animals? How would you explain the possible loss of life it could cause?"

"That can't happen Marcus," replied Nathaniel calmly, "Miranda is completely safe as long as she isn't scared or angered. She is as calm as any other animal I keep here at my home, and as soon as she became accustomed to her cage, she had no problem being fed or examined. As for being parasitic, she feeds on live animals occasionally, latching her mouth upon them somewhere on their bodies, usually in the abdominal area, so that she may have fresh blood from time to time, and I can make that possible by giving her a mouse every once in a while."

This new information did little to calm down the obvious

mild horror upon the faces of the guests, and Samuel decided to give his opinion on the matter, which did little to make him seem brave.

"You cannot keep this creature here in your home Nat! It might escape and find its way into town! I don't want to wake up one morning and find a little blue thing sucking on my bellybutton! Please return it to the desert where it belongs."

"I will not take it back!" barked Nathaniel in return, "Miranda is my new and most beloved pet! I will prove she is harmless!"

Upon stating this, Nathaniel reached down and opened the cage, causing Abigail to faint and both Samuel and Marcus to back away defensively, but these reactions were pointless. Miranda stood there calmly, eyeing the open cage with no interest. She looked as though she had accepted captivity as a retirement from the reality of nature, but upon attempting to close her cage, Nathaniel became quite surprised when she began to charge at the opening as quickly as possible, causing her to slip just barely through, freeing her from her imprisonment. Nathaniel attempted to get a hold of her, but she made her way to the unconscious Abigail, biting ferociously at the linguist's hand like it was fresh ground pork, causing Abigail to awake and claw at Miranda fiercely. Upon being thrust off of Abigail's hand, Miranda made her way to Samuel's ankle, biting down upon it hard. He pulled her off easily, and attempted to carry her back to the cage, but she broke free of his grasp, and fell upon Marcus's shoulder, where in turn she bit onto his neck. Nathaniel then grabbed her by her torso, ripping her off of Marcus, and then causing himself to be bitten on the finger. Yelling in pain, he let Miranda go once more, and she found her way out under the door of the parlor.

Nathaniel now had only the thought of his daughter's safety on his mind, and quickly burst through the door to chase after Miranda before she had a chance to bite Emily. He found Miranda hanging loosely by her remaining teeth off of Emily's arm, as Emily attempted to swing the horrid creature off of her. Nathaniel ripped off the brutal thing, and upon taking it back downstairs to the cage, discovered it was quite injured, and now had dry skin and no teeth left. A loud wind banging against his front doors caused him to break from his curious stare at this oddity of change in Miranda.

"It appears a wind storm has come upon the estate," he said, "so now no one can leave down the road till morning, as it is extremely unsafe. Do not worry; I have many rooms in my house, and I have no reason to reject any of you from being overnight guests. I do need to tell you, however, that a bite from Miranda has a very distasteful effect: the very same substance that is secreted from her skin is also contained in her saliva, and now we have all be quite well dosed with it, so it is now a good time to get some sleep, and hopefully none of you have horrible nightmares about tonight's events, and maybe in the morning we can discuss the changes which have befell Miranda.

"Good night everyone, and let me show you to your rooms."

Part 2: The Dream of Mr. Darlow

Marcus had be taken to a very dark-looking bedroom at the far end of the hall on the second floor of the house by Nathaniel, and was very impressed with the decorating, as he preferred darkness to bright colors when it came to a place to sleep. He undressed, leaving only his undershirt and boxer shorts on, and proceeded, now feeling thoroughly exhausted, under the covers of the large bed, and fell fast asleep, not knowing what was going to come of next morning.

Marcus felt himself awake some time after, noticing that he was no longer in the queen size bed that he had fallen asleep on. An unrecognizable smell wafted past his nose, and he noticed shortly thereafter that he was both blindfolded, and somehow restrained to what felt beneath him as a hardwood table. He could no longer feel his boxer shorts about his lower regions and by that deduced that he was naked. Suddenly, Marcus recognized the now more prevalent smell wafting by his chubby face as warm pecan pie. Marcus now had a watering mouth, and a motivation for getting free of the restraints, but try as he might, they were too great. He lay there, scents changing every so often, making his mouth water more and more. For him it was a true torture, and he wished to eat now so badly that it was killing him inside. He couldn't understand how he got here, but he didn't care. If in the end of this torture he was going to be fed, that was all that mattered.

After what seemed like a day, Marcus finally had his blindfold removed by what appeared to be a man in a black hood and robe. The man spoke with a very deep, intimidating voice that made Marcus feel small and weak.

"Are you hungry? I am sure I can fix you something to eat that you will enjoy; that is if you like meat."

"Please, I am starving," Marcus replied, "all the wonderful smells have made me insatiable. Please feed me something so I may go on."

At this point the man had pulled out a set of large blades, and had started heating up what appeared to be a grill next to the table where Marcus was restrained, but there was no meat nearby, and the man moved the tray of blades next to the table. Handling what appeared to be a bone saw, the hooded man pressed the blade against the flesh just below Marcus's right knee, and began sawing through the bone as quickly as possible. Marcus screamed loudly as the pain registered after a short delay from the shock of his own leg being sawed off. The sound was revolting, and he was beginning to feel himself gag at the possibility of more of his limbs being removed for dastardly and sinister purposes. Once his leg was removed completely, Marcus could feel an incredible burning sensation at the point where it was cut, and realized that the hooded man was cauterizing his wound. He promptly heard a sizzling noise at the grill, and wondered what was being cooked as the intoxicatingly wonderful smell of cooking meat filled his nose.

The hooded man lifted up the leg of Marcus Darlow from the grill, and displayed it to its former owner. Marcus whimpered, and then wondered what he was to be fed. The leg was positioned right over his mouth, and the man spoke again, this time in such a friendly tone it was disgusting.

"Go ahead Marcus; take a bite. It won't kill you. It is quite delicious; I assure you. It will be the only thing you will get to eat for a while. Trust me Marcus." At this point he had no choice but to trust the hooded man that was keeping him restrained, and reluctantly took a bite of his own cooked leg, noticing that it did not taste as good as he had hoped it would, but rather like something one would only eat if it was required of them in an emergency. He finished off as much as he could, with the rest thrown into what sounded like a standard trash bin. He was then promptly blindfolded again, and the intoxicating scents were wafted above him again, making him almost vomit at the prospect of eating again.

What seemed like a couple days passed again before the blindfold was removed for a second time. By this point Marcus had realized that down by his lower regions were holes so that he could possibly relieve himself, and he had done so a couple of times now, not knowing where his excrement was going. The hooded man looked at Marcus with some interest now, and again, without warning, began sawing into the left leg of Marcus Darlow with no hesitation. The pain was again excruciating, but Marcus knew this would be a chance to eat, and regain his strength, but was afraid of what the hooded man would make him eat afterwards. Once his leg was thoroughly cooked, it was offered to him again, and he proceeded to eat it without hesitation, not thinking about what was coming next to aid him in hunger when a few days had passed, not thinking about escape, but only of survival. Once he was finished, the remains were promptly thrown away, and he was again blindfolded.

Days had now passed, and the wonderful scents that filled the air above the table were getting to the mind and sanity of Marcus Darlow, and he began to wonder when again he would possibly get a chance to eat, and for that matter what he was to be fed. After what seemed to be a week he heard various, strange sounds around him, and he was then released from his restraints, and the blindfold removed promptly after. After being sat down at a table by the hooded man, Marcus was given a spoon, and offered a cold beer, which he accepted happily.

The beer was one of the best he had ever tasted, and it made him feel like he was being treated like a human being again. It was a mark of civilization for him, and he was offered another after finishing the first. After accepting his second ale, the hooded man started talking happily.

"We have kept you here now for many days, and you seem to be able to accept the torture like it is a normal everyday thing. As you can see, you have lost a few pounds, and we have decided to give you a reward for being such a good sport. We have the power to return your legs to you, but only after you pass one more test of will, and I assure you, this will not be like consuming your own grilled flesh."

Upon saying it, a bowl was placed in front of Marcus, and the smell coming from it was revolting. Looking down into the bowl, he found out exactly what they had done with his excrement, and it appeared to have been rotting now for many days. He looked up, and the hooded man nodded to him to dig in, and upon looking down again, Marcus felt incredible revulsion. He now had to decide between the ability to walk, or not having to eat his own excrement. The choice was clear, and after going this far, it was time to prove what kind of man he was.

Too hungry to care what was placed in front of him, Marcus Darlow started spooning the rotting feces and urine into his mouth quickly, chewing and swallowing, enjoying every mouthful as though it were the best chocolate mousse, or a well-made beef stew. He couldn't believe what he was missing out on his whole life as he consumed every last bit of his own rotting, disgusting excrement, and upon completion of his meal, burped loudly, signifying that he was content. He placed the spoon down beside the bowl, looked up at the hooded man, and blatantly spoke without thinking about what he was saying, because he was so hungry.

"Can I have some more?"

Part 3: The Dream of Mr. Denny

Samuel was led into one of the more colorful rooms in the Jones house, and he viewed it with pleasure. He was exhausted, and loved bright colors, so after quickly stripping off all of his clothing, Samuel Denny jumped into bed and under the covers, rapidly falling asleep, and hoping he didn't have any strange and eventful dreams.

He awoke to a strange noise coming from outside of what he thought was his room, till he tried to sit up. Something was sealed over him, like the ceiling was dropped down to just inches above his face, and it was making him very uncomfortable. He also noticed that the ceiling, if it had been lowered, was now lined with a very soft material, and he soon started to feel much more comfortable after a bit of getting used to the small space. Samuel was starting to think this was some sort of box, and that maybe he was placed in it as a joke by Nathaniel, or maybe even Marcus, but his ponderings were resolved when the "box" finally opened.

Above him was a gorgeous, naked, and young woman and she climbed in, what Samuel had now realized was a very high end casket, with him, laying directly on top of him, her face directly in front of his, and then the casket shut again, now with what appeared to be a permanent seal, as he could hear sounds of people possibly dropping earth on top of it, and that was when the woman spoke.

"So, what do you think we can do in here with all the time we have? I've had a craving for something a bit naughty, and I was wondering if you would help me." At that, Samuel realized what this young lady wanted, and though it didn't seem the appropriate time, he didn't mind going out with a bang, because if this casket was buried, then who cared about what he and the fox he was with were doing underground.

The two young prisoners underground started having the best sex of their lives, feeling each other's bodies at the closest they ever could; moving back and forth in rhythm, like the way a drummer would play to cause a unit of soldier's to march. Their hearts were beating as fast as a field mouse's would, and they were both shaking with inch insertion and retraction, as though this would be the most perfect moment each time their hips met. To each other, they were the only two people in the world, and there was no reason to waste the last moments they had on this earth being prudes. As it ended they both shook, the perfectly synchronized orgasms making them shiver and quake with ecstasy.

Samuel was sweating profusely now, and he felt incredibly short of breath, which wasn't normal for him. He was known throughout the town for attempting, and usually succeeding, and getting into the underwear of every young girl, for at least three downs past his own. He felt dizzy, and thirsty, but knew there was no water in the casket with him and the beauty that was lying atop of him. Just as he was catching his breath, she spoke again, and what she said was probably something Samuel didn't want to hear, as he had just thought of maybe trying to find a way out.

"Let's do it again. I want some more! I wanna get some more action out of you, you sexy beast!" His reply was immediate, and as quiet as possible.

"I'm dizzy and tired, and I think we are running out of air. If we fuck again, we might suffocate right in the middle of it, and I don't want to die suffocating in a casket underground, let alone during sex with a woman I don't really know"

"I want more, and if you won't give it to me, then I will take it!" After hearing that, Samuel had just realized that maybe he shouldn't have said no. She began to ride him hard and fast, and as he became erect again inside her, it was clear that he was going to be in some pain very soon. She refused to stop, and her movements were now making him hurt around his hip area. After what seemed like eternity, she peaked with gratification, and as her body shook on top of his, Samuel was relieved, especially when he noticed she was dripping with an immense amount of sweat. He was, unfortunately, deprived of that relief, as she screamed loudly then started up again, and without even a word of protest, he passed out.

When Samuel awoke he was still in the casket, but now it appeared to be open to the night sky, and he was having trouble feeling both his genitals and his legs, but he couldn't seem to sit up, so he just lied there. He was relieved to find that the nymphomaniac he was locked in the casket with was apparently gone, and hoped she had quit after the third time. As he lay still, he began to feel his lower back come out of a numbness, and began to sit up, revealing the most horrible thing he had ever seen in his life.

When looking upon his lower regions, Samuel Denny was shocked to discover that his legs were almost beaten raw, as though they had been impacted over and over again for hours. His penis was only just partially intact, and blood was coming out of the end of it, as its main blood vessel had appeared to have broken open slightly. His testicles had exploded, and they were bleeding profusely upon the bottom of the casket, but this was not the last of the horror that was coming upon him as he looked down at his lower regions. The girl that had raped him thoroughly enough to cause the damage that he was looking upon was licking up the blood and semen mix that was covering his mutilated genitalia, and terrifyingly for Samuel, he couldn't feel anything that had been done to him. Noticing the apparent horror on his face, the young woman, who now had aged to what apparently was approximately 105 years in age, looked up at him affectionately, and spoke to him sweetly, as though this was perfectly normal.

"What's wrong baby? I just wanted as much as you could give me, and you know what I think? I think we can go again! I want more! I want more!"

Part 4: The Dream of Miss Lemming

Abigail was taken to a room very close to Emily's, and found herself quite enamored with the quarters with which she had been provided. It didn't take her long to strip down to nothing, as was her preferred choice of sleeping attire, and she proceeded to lie down on top of all the covers, promptly passing out.

She came to in what appeared to be an operating room. She was restrained, as she could feel by her wrists and ankles, and she was still naked, which caused great concern in the head of Miss Lemming. Questions began to surface in her mind, and she wondered why she was in such a place, with no recollection of leaving Nathaniel's home. This, she thought, was going to assuredly be a frightening experience.

Her questions were partially answered when a man in a white lab coat and black mask appeared over her, and she realized she didn't hear him come in. He stood over her, now a scalpel in hand, and that is when she noticed something that now concerned her.

The man was speaking. His lips were moving, but for poor Abigail, nothing was being said. She couldn't hear what he was saying. For the first time in her life, Abigail was concerned about her auditory faculties. She couldn't understand why she had become suddenly deaf, and with such fear she attempted to break free of her restraints, but failed miserably.

The man above her had just started cutting. She could feel the flesh around her navel being split open by the razor sharp scalpel, but she refused to scream. If I scream, she thought, I will only give him that satisfaction. She had seen these kinds of things on television before, and wasn't going to let some sick bastard with some doctor tools get his jollies off of her in pain.

After cutting out Abigail's navel area, the man proceeded

down into her abdomen, now slicing through the viscera towards her intestines. Still refusing to scream, she laid there, taking every last cut. When he reached her intestines, he stopped, and proceeded to her vagina now, scalpel directly thrusted into her clitoris. At this point, Abigail Lemming decided it was time to scream.

She couldn't scream. In fact, she couldn't open her mouth at all. With her tongue she attempted to feel her lips, but instead felt a new wall of flesh. She couldn't communicate; all she could do was breathe and hope that this would be over soon.

After finishing the removal of Abigail's clitoris, the man proceeded to now slice through the bottoms of her breasts, finally cutting them off after several minutes of dissection. She had a distinct look of agony on her face, and the flesh over her mouth and ears was beginning to turn red with the rest of her face. He couldn't believe the perfection of the body he was working on, and how wonderfully beautiful this poor girl was before he began. He wondered how wonderful her eyes would look in his collection, and proceeded to remove one without any problems. It was such a nice eye after all. Now, he thought, time to see what is going through her head.

Abigail screamed inside her mind as the man sawed through the top of her skull. With its removal, she realized this was probably the end of her life. No longer would she study and gain the knowledge to teach and communicate with the rest of the world. With a short look at Miss Lemming's brain, the man picked up a bottle of acid, and proceeded to poor it into her skull. Well, this looks like pudding now, he thought, as she convulsed in wretched horror.

Part 5: The Dream of Mr. Jones

Upon returning to his room for the night, Nathaniel changed into his pajamas, had himself a shot of rum, and proceeded to bed, with his last thought before falling unconscious being one of wonder at the actions of Miranda that very night.

He found himself in his own private study, waking at his

desk, and still in his pajamas. Laying on the floor of his study he saw, and was quite surprised by, a woman, around his age, and naked, slumbering happily. He had no doubt that this was going to be a very interesting thing to explain when she awoke, and he wondered how he came to be in his study, with a strange woman on his floor.

As he pondered his transportation through the house, the woman began to stir, and as she awoke, Nathaniel noticed something strange about her; she appeared to have multicolored hair, of every shade. This oddity was almost unnoticeable when, after finally sitting up, she spoke to Nathaniel.

"Well, I seem to have lost my clothes. Nathaniel, would you do me the honor of finding me some; I feel a bit chilly. I will be quite appreciative." At that, Nathaniel took off his pajama shirt, and handed it over to the woman, and pondered how someone he had never met before could possibly know his name. She put the shirt on, and after standing up, walked over and locked the study door after briefly opening it, and determining that no one was around. She walked back over to Nathaniel, and proceeded to speak again.

"Oh, Nathaniel, I need something from you. I have this problem; this sickness, it plagues me. I need you to help me with it Nathaniel. I want you to help me." He was completely entranced, and couldn't help mumbling; he was under her spell. As he fell to her sorcery, she walked over to the menagerie room, and after going inside for a few minutes, returned with one of the dogs that Nathaniel used as a protective measure while going on desert walks. She tied the dog's chain to one of the tables, and walked back up to Nathaniel, which caused him great joy, so much so all he could do was mumble.

Ripping off his pajama pants revealed that he was, to put it more appropriately, completely excited. She teased him, and so much so that he was having trouble standing, and after 30 minutes or so, being pleased with his ability to restrain himself, she bent over in front of him, and asked him for something important.

"Oh, Nathaniel, make me yours, fuck me hard Nathaniel. I want this pain to go away Nathaniel. Fuck me, and make it go away. You can do it." At the requests of the strange woman, Nathaniel was too intoxicated by her to not say "no", and proceeded to thrust into her, without any restraint whatsoever. I want this, he thought to himself, I want this and I will take it without any hesitation. Her body, her curves controlled him now, and after an hour or so of sexual ecstasy on the part of participating individuals, the woman now had a much more different and intriguing request, or at least intriguing to the hypnotized Nathaniel.

"Go fuck the dog Nathaniel. Shove your cock inside her. You can do it, Nathaniel. I'm begging you please. It is the only way to get rid of my sickness. Make her howl for me Nathaniel." He had to oblige, it was want she wanted, so without any hesitation, Nathaniel Jones stumbled over, and thrust himself into a member of the canine species.

If the visual isn't that astounding, or for that matter you are currently wondering how someone shoves an erect penis into a German Sheppard, I would like to note that it is not that difficult, and Nathaniel had found this out quite immediately. He continued to thrust back and forth inside the poor animal, and as she (the dog) cried out, and as she (the woman) orgasmed heavily from the cries of the dog, Nathaniel proceeded to orgasm inside the poor animal, and as he pulled himself out of her without any obstacles, or for that matter now no reservations, he did something he never thought he would do in his life.

Nathaniel screamed.

Part 6: The Dream of Miss Jones

Emily Jones was not at all tired once the party had dissolved, but after reading a few chapters of her favorite book, she was all at once exhausted, and proceeded into falling asleep in her not so favorite night gown.

Emily found herself in the cemetery. She was still in her nightgown, and it was the middle of the night, so she shivered vigorously. Walking in between the headstones, Emily wondered how she had gotten here, and why she was dressed so lightly in such cold weather. As she walked around, she realized that she was in the area of the cemetery where her own mother was buried. Surprisingly enough, she ended up at her mother's grave to be shocked.

The grave was empty. A hole where the green soft grass had been, and the casket which had held her mother's body was now open. Emily was now scared; who would be willing to take out the corpse of a mother that had died so young? A necrophiliac? A Satanist? She hoped her questions would never be answered, and that she could leave this place without ever finding out, but unfortunately the questions answered themselves.

Standing behind poor Emily was her mother, Amelia, but instead of having normal human posture and cleanliness, she had dirty hands, the dress she had been buried in was filthy, her hair was matted, her skin rotting, and her face was oozing pus, with her mouth a gaping, toothless hole. Then Emily turned around.

Looking upon her deceased mother, she discovered the rotting, stinking, decayed corpse was the greatest thing she had ever seen since the day Amelia Jones had died, and without a second thought at her mother's appearance, ran up and hugged the corpse. For the first time in a long time, Emily Jones was completely happy. Nothing could make this moment less memorable; her mother was back from the dead. She spoke to the cadaver, hoping to take it with her.

"Come with me mommy. We can go home, and you and Dad and I can all live together, and take care of the animals, and we can live happily ever after. Please, let's leave this place." The body of her mother said nothing, only breathing heavily, and after a minute or so of staring, something horrid began to happen.

Amelia's mouth began to form sharp, yellowed fangs, as though they had retracted into her jaw, and she grabbed Emily, holding her while attempting to bite through to the young girl's body. Emily loosened herself from the corpse's grip, and began to run.

The cemetery seemed endless, and every time she looked back, she could see her mother catching up to her, fangs still glowing in the dark. There was no escaping such a monster, Emily thought, but she continued to run, hoping that she would find her way out before her mother could catch her. Unfortunately, for Emily, where there is one corpse-monster-thing, there is probably another.

Another corpse appeared in front of Miss Jones, and without a doubt that this was going to be a fight for her life, she turned and continued to run. After about a 100 yards, another cadaver appeared, and she now had no doubt that escape was impossible.

Sitting on the ground, the corpses began to tear through her clothes and flesh, their rotting smell permeating her innocence and ignorance, and before she could even scream for her father, her mother ripped out her lung.

And that is when she woke up.

Part 7: Nightmarish Conclusion

Walking through the eerily silent house, Emily at once realized that the nightmare she had experienced must have been caused by some intoxicant, or other inebriating device, but couldn't explain to herself how such a thing came to be in her system. As she paced the house, she wondered to herself if any of the other occupants had suffer similar consequences, and to what end did they too find themselves drugged.

Upon leaving her bedroom, she first walked over to the closest bathroom, hoping to wash off the horrid hallucination she had been a part of, and to attempt to clean away all her troubles or cares. It was when opening the door did she realize the full effect of the bite of Miranda, for sitting with his head in the toilet, dead, and in a most relaxed position, was Mr. Darlow, and upon looking down into the porcelain death-trap that he had supposedly been placed in, she saw that his mouth was fully open, and that inside of it were his own feces, which he appeared to be eating with relish.

After vomiting profusely next to Mr. Darlow's corpse, she wrenched herself from the bathroom, and continued to proceed down the upstairs hall, to find the door to Miss Lemming's room ajar. Upon further inspection, she saw that Miss Lemming was kneeling on the floor, crying, and holding her ears, which, by the brown stains, had been apparently bleeding, and Miss Lemming had made an attempt to stop the flow of life that was coming from her delicate auditory receptors. Emily walked up to her, and made a comforting gesture, but Abigail promptly shooed her away, and even started violently pushing her out of the bedroom, at which point Emily walked out.

Emily continued downstairs to find Mr. Denny naked at the foot of them, which puzzled her so. Trying not to embarrass him, she politely announced she was coming down, and he looked up, oddly, with a smile, and spoke.

"Ah, Emily. How are you doing this morning?" he said.

"I'm fine Mr. Denny. How are you doing?" she replied.

"Oh, I just had the worst nightmare of my life. You?"

"Yes. Do you know why this has happened?"

"It was that damned Miranda. Your father was foolish to bring such a creature into his home. I see you are wearing a robe. May I have it? I will buy you a new one. This blasted nakedness is getting to me." She then handed him her robe, which, although it was rather small, covered him up quite suitably, and together they walked off on the bottom floor to look for her father.

They found him in his private study. He was hunched over his desk, looking quite sick, and it was obvious he had vomited all over himself. A number of papers on his desk were scribbled upon hastily. His disheveled appearance caused Samuel to speak.

"Nat, are you alright" he said.

"I am fine Sam. Just sick, that's all. Would you look in that cage for me?" he replied, and pointed over to a cage on the shelf. Samuel looked, and replied most quickly.

"It's empty Nat. It's just an empty cage"

"Good," replied Nathaniel, "I am happy we are free of that damned creature. I no doubt believe you are just as excited. She made me fuck my dog for God's sake."

www.ingramcontent.com/pod-product-compliance
Ingram Content Group UK Ltd.
Pitfield, Milton Keynes, MK11 3LW, UK
UKHW041929190726
13854UKWH00004B/1529

9 781105 101885